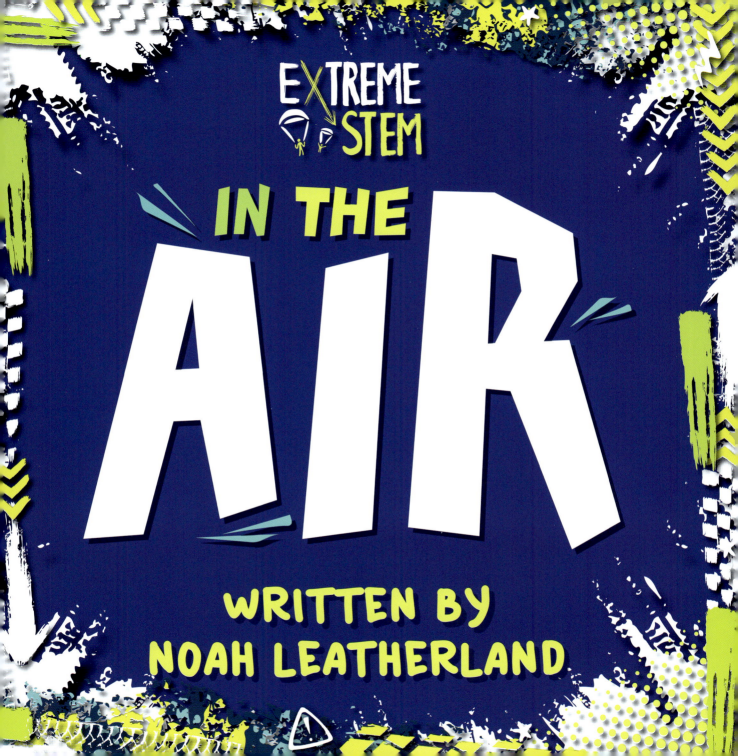

In the Air © 2024 BookLife Publishing
This edition is published by arrangement with BookLife Publishing

sales@northstareditions.com
888-417-0195

Library of Congress Control Number: 2025930424

ISBN
979-8-89359-313-6 (library bound)
979-8-89359-397-6 (paperback)
979-8-89359-371-6 (epub)
979-8-89359-343-5 (hosted ebook)

Printed in the United States of America
Mankato, MN
092025

Written by:
Noah Leatherland

Edited by:
Rebecca Phillips-Bartlett

Designed by:
Amelia Harris

American adaptation copyright © 2026 by North Star Editions, Mendota Heights, MN 55120. All rights reserved. No part of this book may be reproduced or utilized in any form or by any means without written permission from the publisher.

All facts, statistics, web addresses and URLs in this book were verified as valid and accurate at time of writing. No responsibility for any changes to external websites or references can be accepted by either the author or publisher.

Image Credits

Images are courtesy of Shutterstock.com. With thanks to Getty Images, Thinkstock Photo and iStockphoto. Cover – Sky Antonio. Recurring Images – Doctor Letters, Arak Rattanawijittakorn, Double Brain, hasfungraphics, Matisson_ART, topform, wow.subtropica, Zoa.Arts. 2–3 – ynm_yn. 4–5 – Lucian BOLCA, wavebreakmedia. 6–7 – EB Adventure Photography, VO IMAGES. 8–9 – Pepermpron, Kapustin Igor, Anshuman Rath. 10–11 – goffkein.pro, Nick Rostov. 12–13 – DedMityay, Valentina Vectors. 14–15 – Michaelvbg, Rick Neves. 16–17 – Rick Neves, AlejandroCarnicero. 18–19 – NASA ID: S85-44834, Public domain via Wikimedia Commons, PLBechly, CC BY-SA 4.0 via Wikimedia Commons. 20–21 – HN Works, HN Works. 22–23 – Joggie Botma, Mauricio Graiki.

Contents

PAGE 4 — Extreme STEM

PAGE 6 — Helicopters

PAGE 10 — Hot-Air Balloons

PAGE 14 — Wingsuits

PAGE 18 — Zero-Gravity Flights

PAGE 22 — Push the Limits!

PAGE 24 — Glossary and Index

Words that look like THIS can be found in the glossary on page 24.

EXTREME STEM

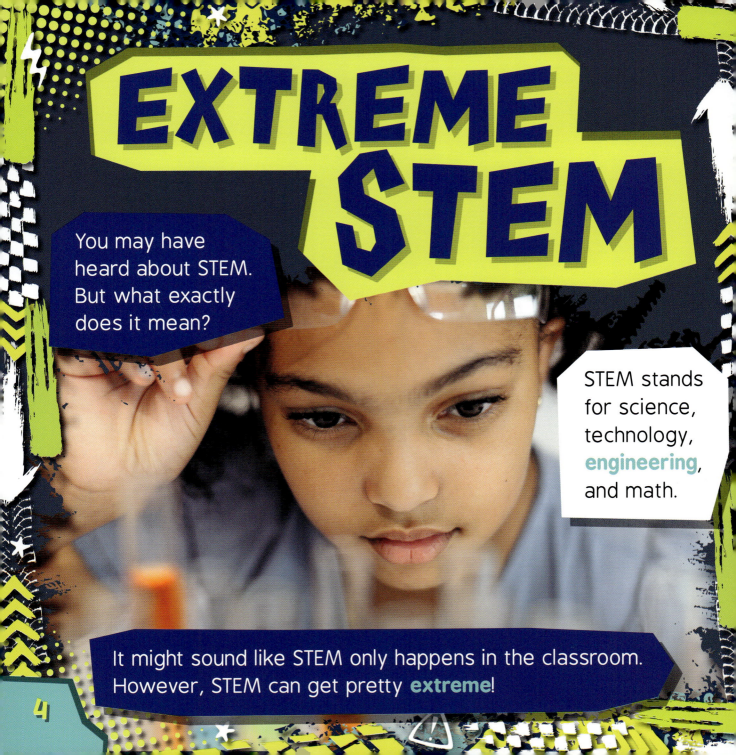

You may have heard about STEM. But what exactly does it mean?

STEM stands for science, technology, **engineering**, and math.

It might sound like STEM only happens in the classroom. However, STEM can get pretty **extreme**!

HIGH IN THE SKY

People can't fly on their own. But they can soar through the sky using the power of STEM.

Are you ready to look at some extreme STEM in the air? Then you better buckle up!

HELICOPTERS

Can you imagine standing still and then rising into the sky? Helicopters do just that. These **vehicles** use spinning blades. They lift off from the ground and fly straight up.

Gravity is a **force**. It pulls things toward the ground. For something to get into the air, it has to push upward with a force stronger than the gravity pulling it down.

LET'S GO FOR A SPIN!

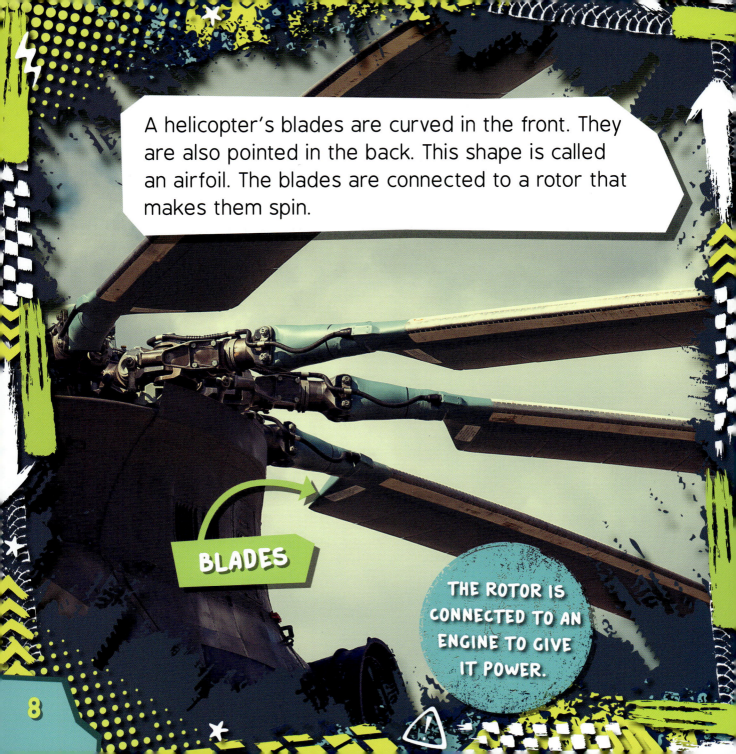

A helicopter's blades are curved in the front. They are also pointed in the back. This shape is called an airfoil. The blades are connected to a rotor that makes them spin.

BLADES

THE ROTOR IS CONNECTED TO AN ENGINE TO GIVE IT POWER.

When an airfoil moves quickly, some air moves over it. Some air moves under it. This movement creates an upward force called lift. Helicopter blades create enough lift to raise the helicopter into the air.

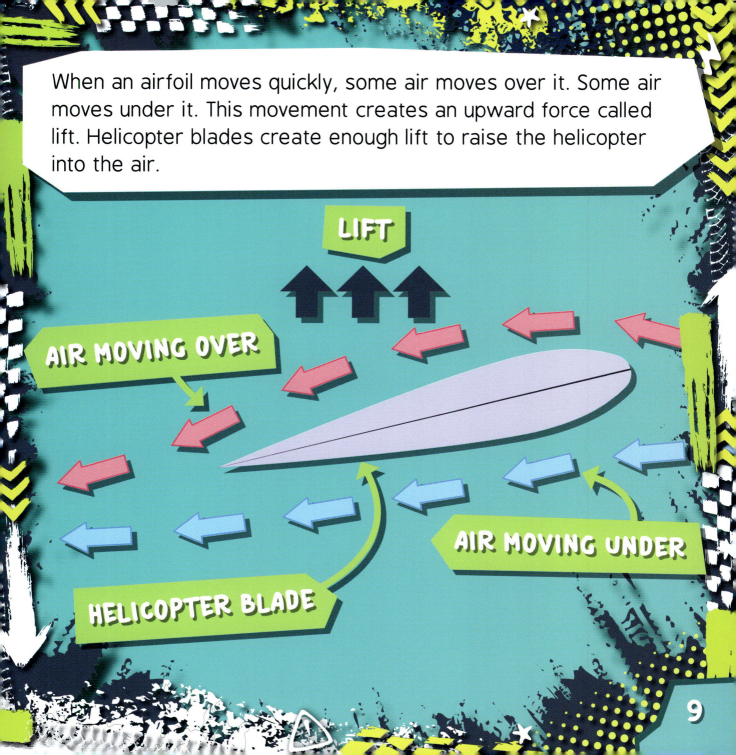

HOT-AIR BALLOONS

People have been riding in hot-air balloons for more than 200 years. Hot-air balloons were one of the first ways that people figured out how to fly.

Hot-air balloons might look peaceful moving slowly in the sky. However, it doesn't get much more extreme than blasting into the sky using the power of fire!

IT'S TIME TO HEAT THINGS UP!

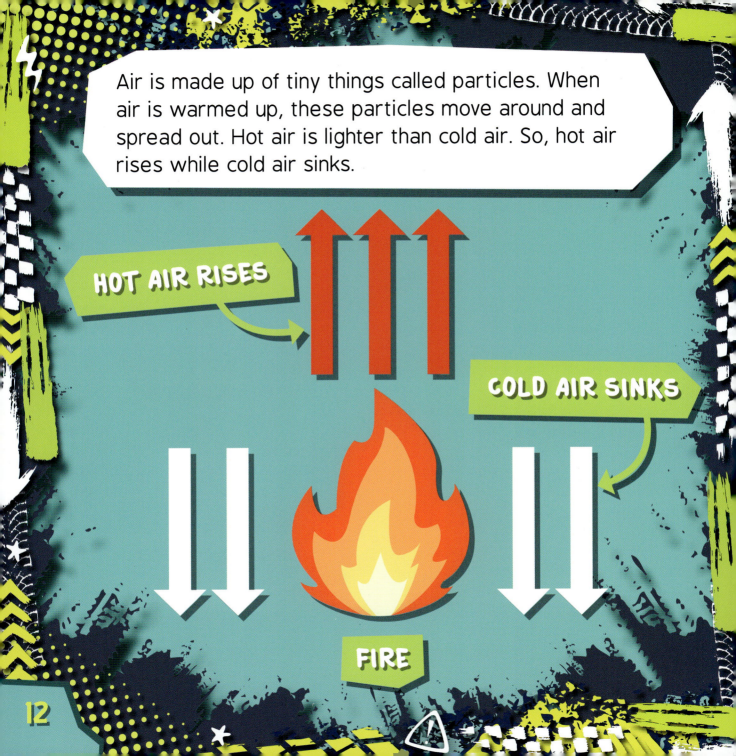

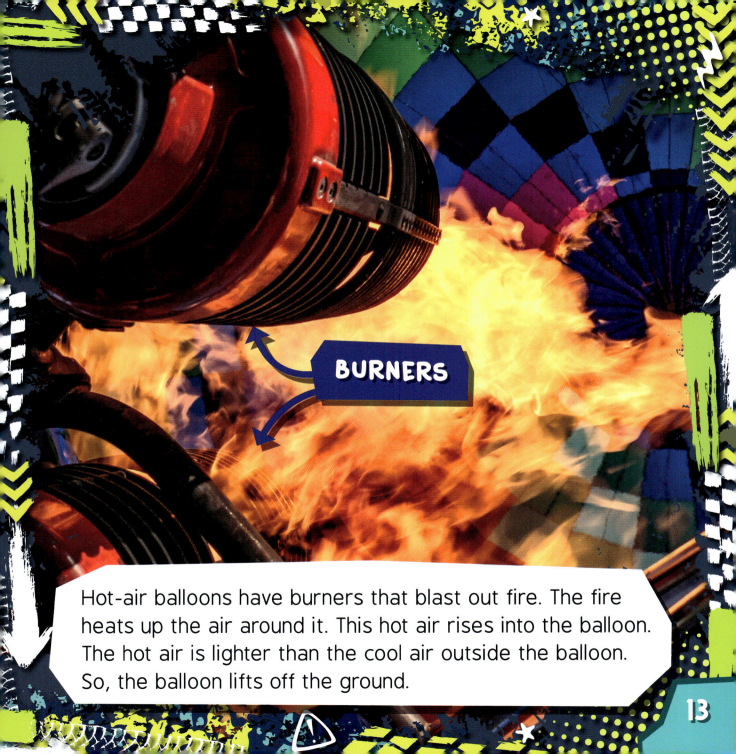

BURNERS

Hot-air balloons have burners that blast out fire. The fire heats up the air around it. This hot air rises into the balloon. The hot air is lighter than the cool air outside the balloon. So, the balloon lifts off the ground.

WINGSUITS

We've seen some ways people use vehicles to fly. But what if someone wanted to fly through the air without a machine?

WINGSUITS ARE AWESOME!

To be totally extreme, they could use a wingsuit.

A wingsuit is a suit designed for jumping from high places. It makes a person into the shape of an airfoil. Fabric spreads out near the person's body.

Wingsuits create lift as they move through the air. As a result, people move forward as they fall. This process is called gliding.

The more lift wingsuits create, the farther people can glide.

Then people use parachutes to land safely. Air hits the underside of the parachute as it falls. This movement creates a force called drag. Drag slows down the parachute.

IT'S STILL A LONG WAY DOWN!

ZERO-GRAVITY FLIGHTS

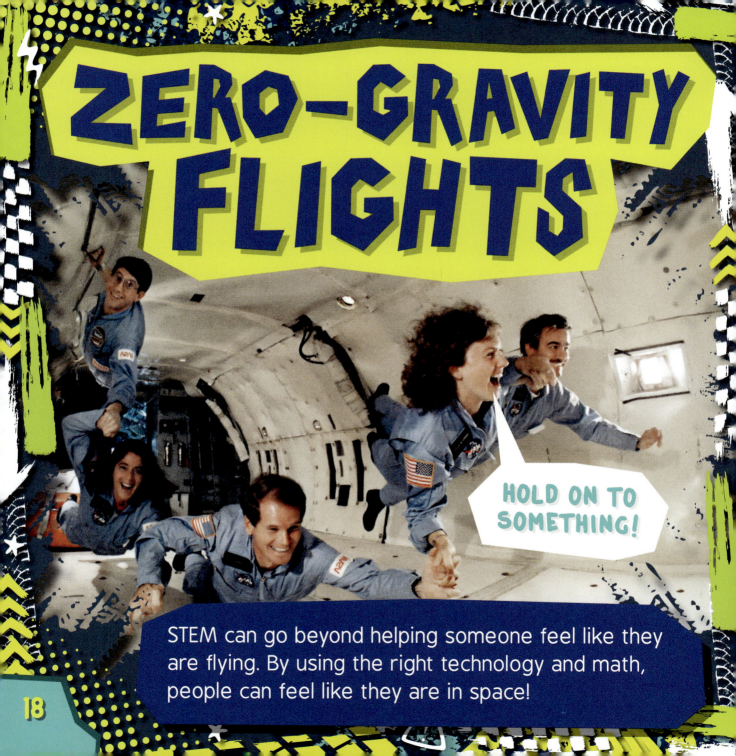

HOLD ON TO SOMETHING!

STEM can go beyond helping someone feel like they are flying. By using the right technology and math, people can feel like they are in space!

Weight is how much gravity acts on an object. Airplanes are not weightless in the sky. However, some planes can fly a certain way to make their passengers feel weightless. This feeling is called zero gravity. It is how people feel in space.

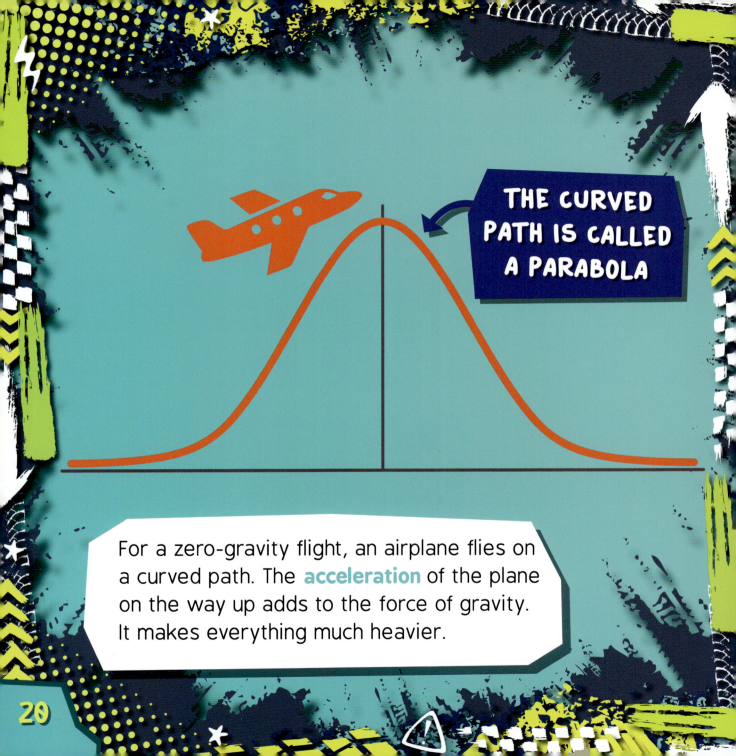

Then the plane slows down near the top of the curve. Passengers are lifted into the air for about 20 seconds. Then the plane goes into **free fall**. The passengers feel weightless!

DOES ANYONE REMEMBER WHICH WAY IS UP?

PUSH THE LIMITS!

See? STEM can be more than just numbers on a page. It can be totally extreme and push the **limits** of what humans can do!

STEM HELPS ME GET EXTREME!

Think of something you might see flying through the air. What forces are acting on it? What parts of STEM might be involved? What technology is being used?

23

GLOSSARY

ACCELERATION — how quickly something is speeding up

ENGINEERING — designing and building machines or structures

EXTREME — much beyond what is usual or expected

FORCE — something that causes an object to move or changes how it moves

FREE FALL — a rapid drop to the ground

LIMITS — the highest levels something can reach

VEHICLES — machines that are used to carry people or things

INDEX

airfoils 8–9, 15
blades 8–9
engines 8
fire 11–13
gravity 7, 19–20
parachutes 17
particles 12
passengers 19, 21